SAXOPHONE PLAY-ALONG

Audio Access Included

PLAYBACK+
Speed · Pitch · Balance · Loop

Dave Koz

T0084242

E♭ Saxophones	B♭ Saxophones	CONTENTS
2	29	All I See Is You
8	32	Can't Let You Go (The Sha La Song)
12	36	Emily
5	40	Honey-Dipped
16	46	Know You by Heart
26	43	Put the Top Down
18	48	Together Again
22	52	You Make Me Smile

To access audio visit:
www.halleonard.com/mylibrary

Enter Code
6506-8158-1892-6225

Cover photo by John M. Heller/Getty Images

ISBN: 978-1-4803-3799-2

Visit Hal Leonard Online at
www.halleonard.com

cherry lane
music company

EXCLUSIVELY DISTRIBUTED BY
HAL•LEONARD®
CORPORATION
7777 W. BLUEMOUND RD. P.O. BOX 13819 MILWAUKEE, WI 53213

All I See Is You

By Dave Koz and Brian Culbertson

Eb Sax

Eb Sax

Honey-Dipped

By Dave Koz and Jeff Lorber

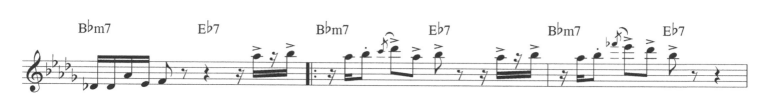

Begin fade

Fade out

Eb Sax

Can't Let You Go
(The Sha La Song)
By Dave Koz, Carl Sturken and Evan Rogers

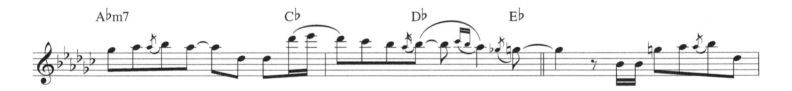

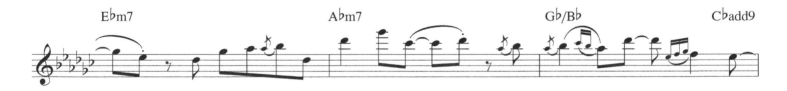

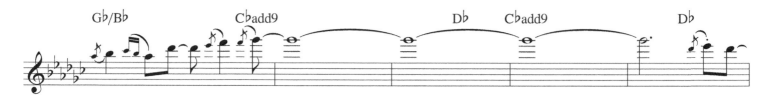

Eb Sax

Emily

By Dave Koz, Jeff Lorber and Bobby Caldwell

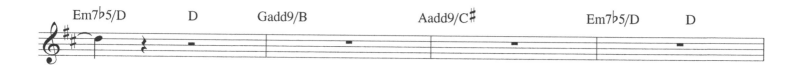

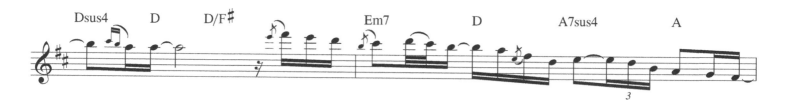

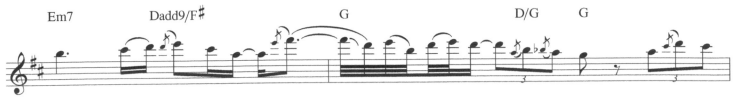

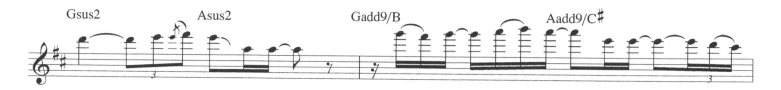

Eb Sax

Know You by Heart

By David Koz and Skip Ewing

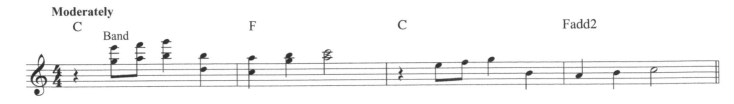

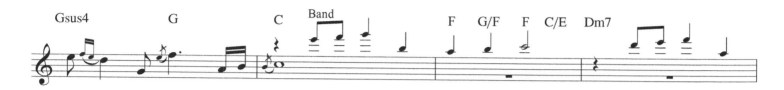

Eb Sax

Together Again

By Dave Koz and Jeff Koz

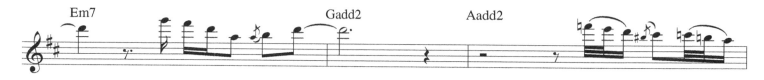

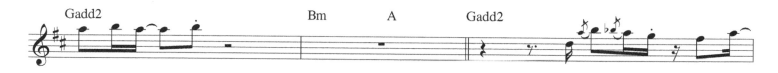

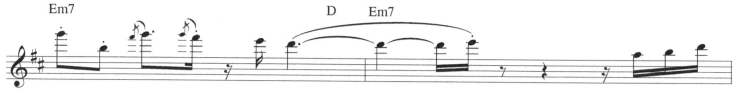

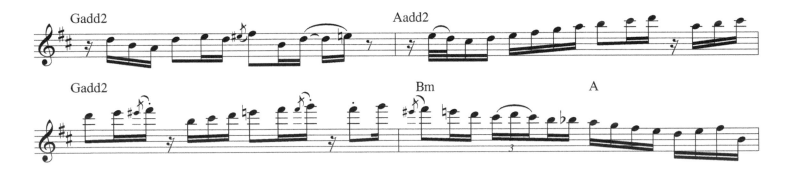

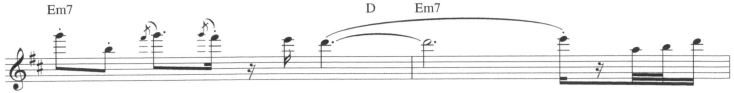

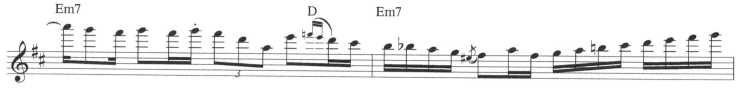

Eb Sax

You Make Me Smile

By Dave Koz and Jeff Koz

Moderately, rhythmic

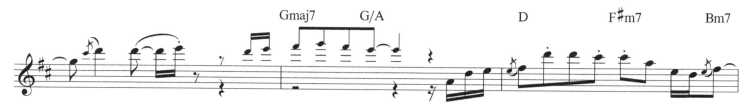

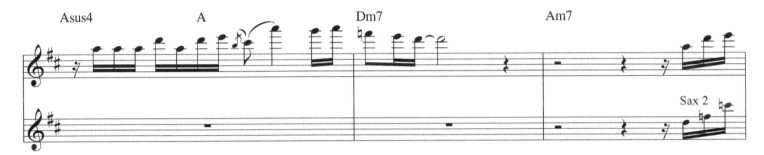

Begin fade

Eb Sax

Put the Top Down

By Dave Koz and Brian Culbertson

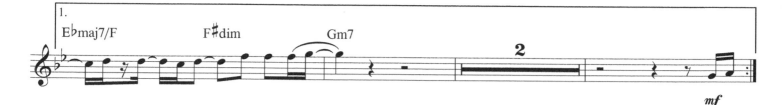

Guitar Solo

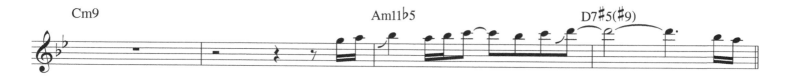

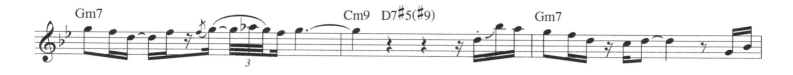

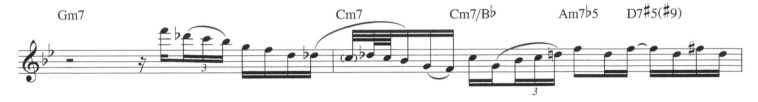

Begin fadeout

All I See Is You

By Dave Koz and Brian Culbertson

Bb Sax

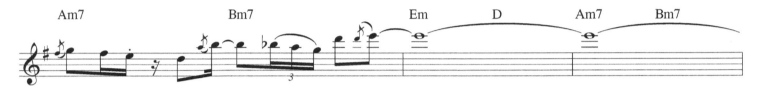

Begin fade

Fade out

Bb Sax

Can't Let You Go
(The Sha La Song)

By Dave Koz, Carl Sturken and Evan Rogers

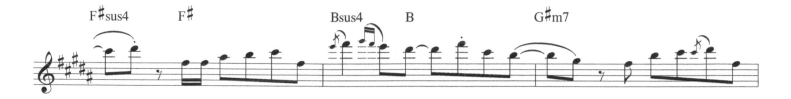

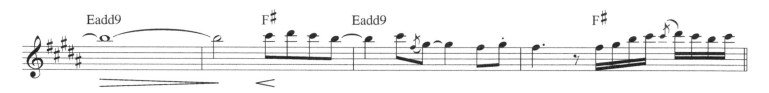

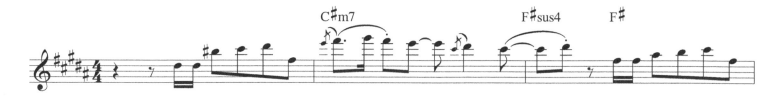

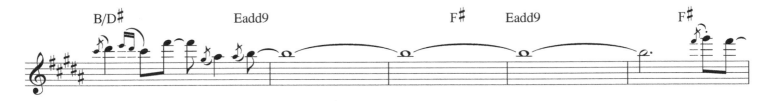

Bb Sax

Emily

By Dave Koz, Jeff Lorber and Bobby Caldwell

Bb Sax

Honey-Dipped

By Dave Koz and Jeff Lorber

Slow Funk beat

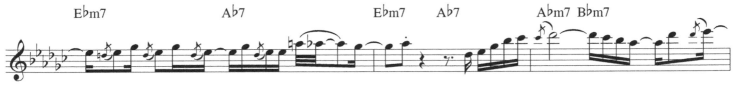

Bb Sax

Put the Top Down

By Dave Koz and Brian Culbertson

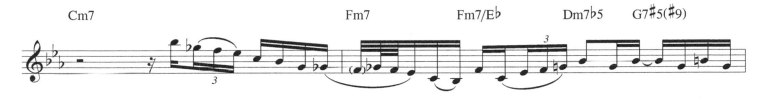

Begin fadeout

Bb Sax

Know You by Heart

By David Koz and Skip Ewing

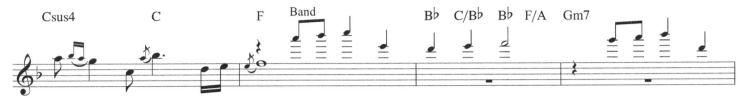

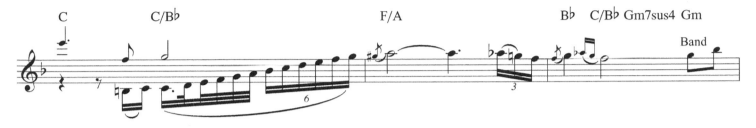

Freely

Bb Sax

Together Again

By Dave Koz and Jeff Koz

Moderately, rhythmic

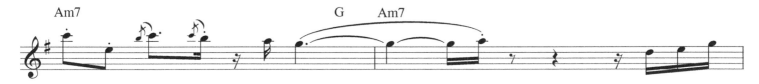

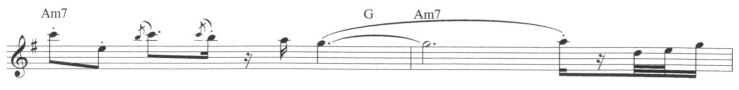

Bb Sax

You Make Me Smile

By Dave Koz and Jeff Koz

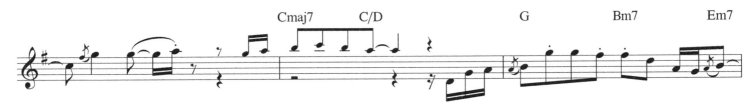

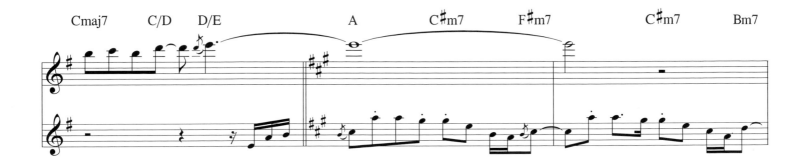

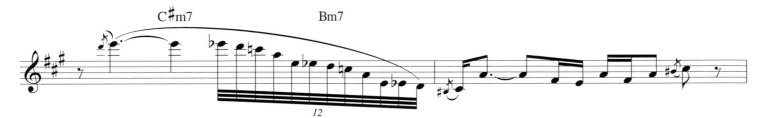

HAL•LEONARD® SAXOPHONE PLAY-ALONG

The Saxophone Play-Along Series will help you play your favorite songs quickly and easily. Just follow the music, listen to the audio to hear how the saxophone should sound, and then play along using the separate backing tracks. Each song is printed twice in the book: once for alto and once for tenor saxes. The online audio is available for streaming or download using the unique code printed inside the book, and it includes **PLAYBACK+** *options such as looping and tempo adjustments.*

1. ROCK 'N' ROLL
Bony Moronie • Charlie Brown • Hand Clappin' • Honky Tonk (Parts 1 & 2) • I'm Walkin' • Lucille (You Won't Do Your Daddy's Will) • See You Later, Alligator • Shake, Rattle and Roll.

00113137 Book/Online Audio $16.99

2. R&B
Cleo's Mood • I Got a Woman • Pick up the Pieces • Respect • Shot Gun • Soul Finger • Soul Serenade • Unchain My Heart.

00113177 Book/Online Audio $16.99

3. CLASSIC ROCK
Baker Street • Deacon Blues • The Heart of Rock and Roll • Jazzman • Smooth Operator • Turn the Page • Who Can It Be Now? • Young Americans.

00113429 Book/Online Audio $16.99

4. SAX CLASSICS
Boulevard of Broken Dreams • Harlem Nocturne • Night Train • Peter Gunn • The Pink Panther • St. Thomas • Tequila • Yakety Sax.

00114393 Book/Online Audio. $16.99

5. CHARLIE PARKER
Billie's Bounce (Bill's Bounce) • Confirmation • Dewey Square • Donna Lee • Now's the Time • Ornithology • Scrapple from the Apple • Yardbird Suite.

00118286 Book/Online Audio $16.99

6. DAVE KOZ
All I See Is You • Can't Let You Go (The Sha La Song) • Emily • Honey-Dipped • Know You by Heart • Put the Top Down • Together Again • You Make Me Smile.

00118292 Book/Online Audio $16.99

7. GROVER WASHINGTON, JR.
East River Drive • Just the Two of Us • Let It Flow • Make Me a Memory (Sad Samba) • Mr. Magic • Take Five • Take Me There • Winelight.

00118293 Book/Online Audio $16.99

8. DAVID SANBORN
Anything You Want • Bang Bang • Chicago Song • Comin' Home Baby • The Dream • Hideaway • Slam • Straight to the Heart.

00125694 Book/Online Audio $16.99

9. CHRISTMAS
The Christmas Song (Chestnuts Roasting on an Open Fire) • Christmas Time Is Here • Count Your Blessings Instead of Sheep • Do You Hear What I Hear • Have Yourself a Merry Little Christmas • The Little Drummer Boy • White Christmas • Winter Wonderland.

00148170 Book/Online Audio $16.99

10. JOHN COLTRANE
Blue Train (Blue Trane) • Body and Soul • Central Park West • Cousin Mary • Giant Steps • Like Sonny (Simple Like) • My Favorite Things • Naima (Niema).

00193333 Book/Online Audio $16.99

11. JAZZ ICONS
Body and Soul • Con Alma • Oleo • Speak No Evil • Take Five • There Will Never Be Another You • Tune Up • Work Song.

00199296 Book/Online Audio $16.99

12. SMOOTH JAZZ
Bermuda Nights • Blue Water • Europa • Flirt • Love Is on the Way • Maputo • Songbird • Winelight.

00248670 Book/Online Audio $16.99

13. BONEY JAMES
Butter • Let It Go • Stone Groove • Stop, Look, Listen (To Your Heart) • Sweet Thing • Tick Tock • Total Experience • Vinyl.

00257186 Book/Online Audio $16.99